CLOSE-UP

OCEAN LIFE

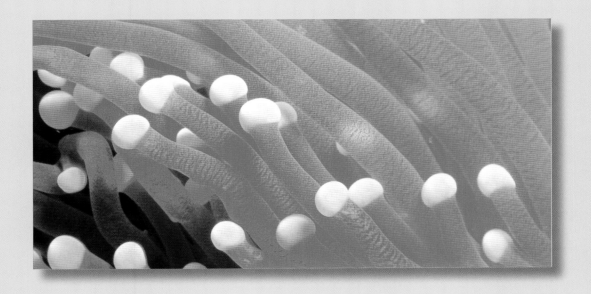

BROWN
BEAR
BOOKS

Published by Brown Bear Books Limited

An imprint of
The Brown Reference Group plc
68 Topstone Road
Redding
Connecticut
06896
USA
www.brownreference.com

ISBN: 978-1-93383-416-0

Authors: John Woodward and Leon Gray
Designer: Lynne Lennon
Picture Researcher: Rupert Palmer
Managing Editor: Bridget Giles
Production Director: Alastair Gourlay
Children's Publisher: Anne O'Daly

Picture credits
Front cover: Science Photo Library: Susumu Nishinaga
Title page: Shutterstock.com: WizData Inc.
Science Photo Library: Eye of Science 27, Steve Gshmeissner 9, Manfred Kage
7, D. Roberts 23, Alexis Rosenfeld 11, Susumu Nishinaga 29, David Scharf 25,
Peter Scoones 21, Andrew Syred 5, 13, 15; Shutterstock.com: WizData Inc. 19;
Superstock: age Fotostock 17.

Library of Congress Cataloging-in-Publication Data

Ocean life.

    p. cm. – (Close-up)

Includes bibliographical references and index.

ISBN-13: 978-1-933834-16-0 (alk. paper)

1. Marine animals–Juvenile literature.

QL122.2 .O293 2007

591.77 22

2006103053

Printed in China
9 8 7 6 5 4 3 2 1

Contents

Ocean Food

Earth's huge oceans are full of tiny creatures called plankton. There are many thousands of types of plankton. They come in different shapes and sizes. Most plankton are so small they can only be seen using a microscope or magnifying glass.

On the Seafloor

Plantlike plankton called diatoms have hard shells made from a chemical called silica. When the diatoms die and rot away, the silica is all that is left. The silica collects on the seafloor as a white sandy powder.

Plant plankton

Some plankton are like animals and eat other creatures. Other plankton are more like plants. Many larger sea creatures would die if there were no plantlike plankton in the oceans. Some sea animals eat this plankton. Others eat the animals that feed on the plantlike plankton.

Seashell Spirals

Some plankton are like animals because they feed on other creatures. Some animal-like plankton have hard chalky shells that protect their soft insides. One of these plankton is called *Globigerina*.

Shell spaces

Globigerina grows as a round shell. As the creature gets bigger, it makes more round shells. The shells form in a spiral shape. The spiral is surrounded by long spines. The shells and spines contain a liquid that makes *Globigerina* float in the water.

Marine Ooze

When *Globigerina* dies, its empty shell falls to the seafloor. When the shell breaks up, it forms a chalky mud called marine ooze. The ooze covers the seafloor. In some places, it is hundreds of feet thick.

This picture shows a group of round Globigerina shells. The surface of each shell is full of tiny holes. The Globigerina takes in food through the holes in the shell.

Glassy Sculpture

Many plantlike plankton are called diatoms. Like most land plants, diatoms contain a green coloring called chlorophyll. The chlorophyll helps diatoms trap energy from the Sun. Diatoms use this energy to make food. Since they need the Sun to make their food, diatoms float near the top of the seawater.

Plankton Fuel

When plankton die, they sink to the seabed. The dead bodies break up and form a fine mud. Over millions of years, layer upon layer of plankton mud builds up on the ocean floor. The weight of the top layers of mud presses down on the lower layers. This pressure changes the mud into oil and gas.

Silica shapes

Diatoms are made up of one cell. The cell has two parts. One part fits the other like a lid on a box. The cell's wall is a hard, glassy chemical called silica. The cell walls of some diatoms form interesting shapes and patterns.

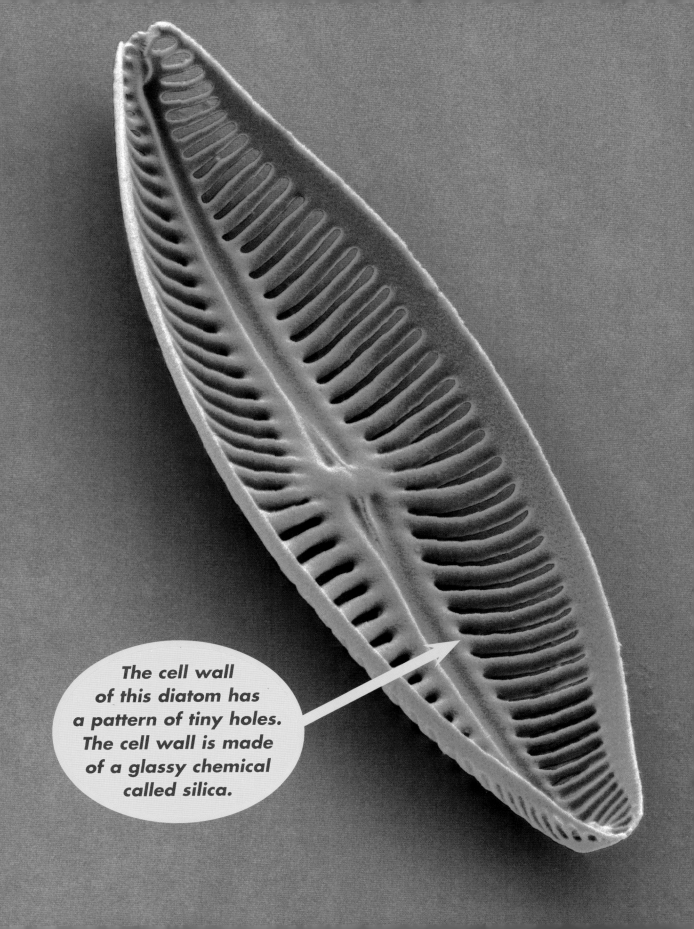

Shark Tale

Most fish have a skeleton made of hard bone. These fish are called bony fish. A shark's bones are made of a rubbery substance called cartilage. Sharks are known as cartilaginous fish. You have cartilage in your nose and ears!

Inside or out?

Bony fish lay eggs in the water. The eggs float until they are ready to hatch into small fish. Most sharks come from eggs that grow inside the mother's body. When the young shark is born, it looks like a tiny version of its mother.

Shark King

The whale shark is the biggest shark and the biggest of all the fish. An adult whale shark measures about 50 feet (15 meters) in length. Whale sharks eat plankton and small fish.

A dogfish's egg case. The dogfish is a small shark. Unlike most sharks, the female dogfish lays her egg in an egg case. The young dogfish hatches after 9 months.

Speedy Swimmers

Squid belong to a group of animals called mollusks. Mollusks have soft bodies and a hard shell. A squid's shell is inside it's body. Some mollusks, such as snails, live on the land. Most, such as squid, live in the sea.

Great Lengths

Of all the thousands of types of animals without a backbone, the giant squid is the largest. It grows up to 55 feet (17 meters) long. Most squid are much smaller. They grow up to 12 inches (30 centimeters) long.

Fast swimmers

Over short distances, squid are among the fastest ocean swimmers. The long body of the squid is streamlined. That means it is well shaped for swimming. When a squid needs to swim fast, it forces a jet of water out of a tube in its body. This jet propels the squid out of danger at top speed.

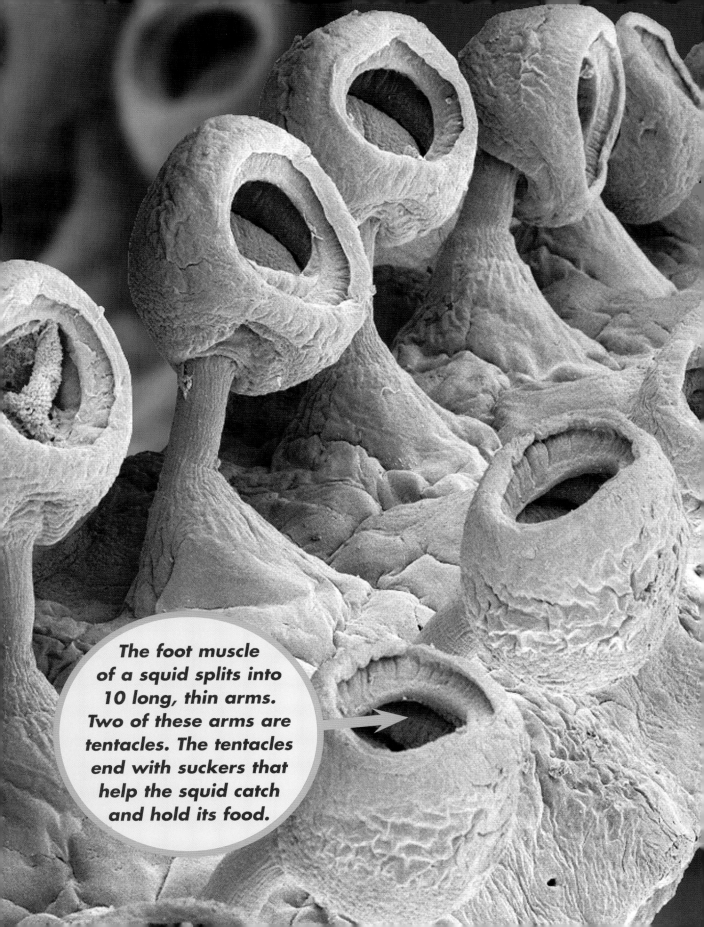

The foot muscle of a squid splits into 10 long, thin arms. Two of these arms are tentacles. The tentacles end with suckers that help the squid catch and hold its food.

Whelk Warriors

A dog whelk is a mollusk. It has a soft body and a hard, pointed shell. Dog whelks live under rocks on beaches. The female lays her eggs in a long egg case. When the eggs hatch, the young whelks crawl out and cling to a nearby rock.

Tongue teeth

Barnacles are the dog whelk's favorite food. The whelk uses its long tongue to drill through a barnacle's hard shell. The tongue has rows of sharp teeth that scrape food from inside the shell.

Changing Teeth

A whelk grows new teeth when the old teeth wear out. The new teeth move up from the back of the tongue to replace the worn teeth in front.

A dog whelk's tongue is covered with rows of sharp teeth. The whelk uses its teeth to scrape food into small pieces so it can swallow them.

Fan-shaped Beauties

A scallop is a mollusk. It has a soft body and two fan-shaped shells joined on one side by a hinge. One shell is rounded and the other is flat. Scallop shells come in many beautiful patterns and dazzling colors.

Eyes and Mouth

Although a scallop has eyes and a mouth, it does not have a head! The tiny eyes are found on the edges of the scallop's shells. The mouth is a hole that opens directly into the body. The scallop eats by sucking food through the hole.

Scallop stroke

Scallops can swim by clapping their shells together. This forces out a jet of water. The water jet pushes the scallop through the sea. Scallops swim to find food and to escape enemies such as starfish.

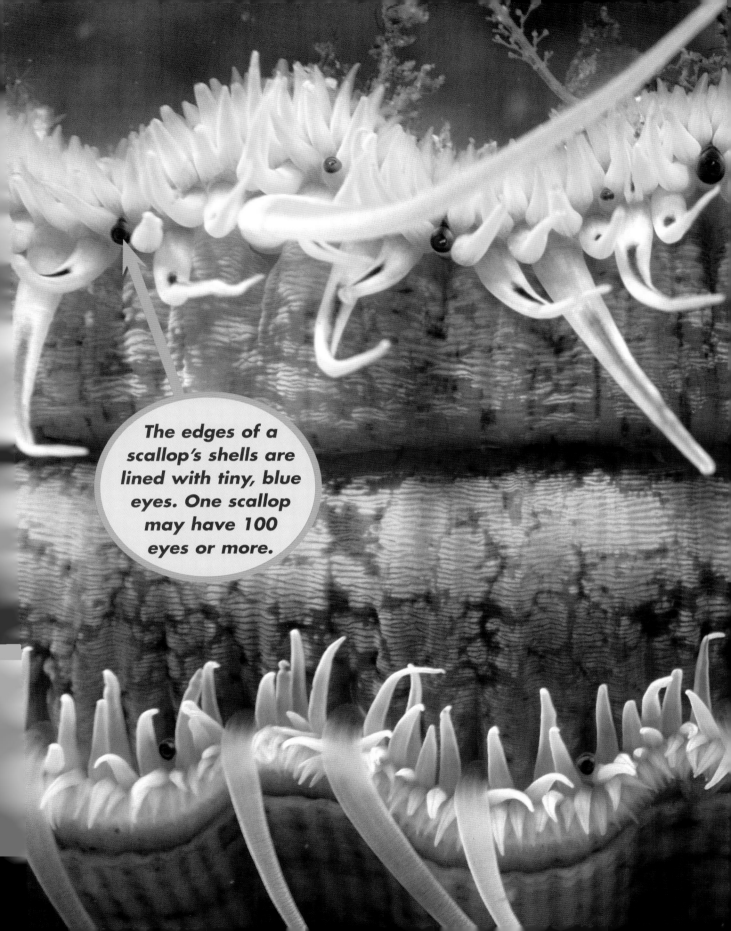

The edges of a scallop's shells are lined with tiny, blue eyes. One scallop may have 100 eyes or more.

Sea Stingers

Sea anemones look like plants, but they are animals. Sea anemones live on rocks under the sea. They slide around very slowly and eat other sea animals that pass close to their stinging arms.

Deadly anemone

A sea anemone's arms surround the animal's mouth. The body looks like a blob of gelatin. When the sea anemone's stinging arms are extended, it looks like a pretty underwater flower. But it is a deadly predator of shrimps and other sea creatures.

Stinging Cells

Each of the sea anemone's arms has a small U-shaped part that contains a stinging cell. When an animal swims into the center of the sea anemone, the anemone uses these stingers to stun its prey. The anemone then drags its meal to the hole that leads to the stomach.

The arms of this sea anemone end with tiny stinging cells. The stingers stun small sea animals so the sea anemone can swallow them whole.

Sea Hedgehogs

Sea urchins belong to the same group of animals as starfish. This group is the echinoderms, which means "hedgehog spines." All echinoderms have hard shells covered with spines. The shell protects the echinoderm's soft insides. The spines protect the animal from attackers.

Unusual Food

Some people eat sea urchins. Japanese and Korean chefs sometimes cook parts of male sea urchins. The flesh looks like a firm orange or yellow "custard."

Life on the seafloor

Sea urchins usually live on loose rocks at the bottom of the ocean. In stormy seas, sea urchins cling tightly to the rocks. Sometimes sea urchins move closer to the beach. They move using hundreds of tiny sticky feet on the bottom of their bodies.

Shell Test

Scientists call the sea urchin's hard shell a "test." One type of sea urchin has a round shell with a flat bottom. The sea urchin's mouth lies in the middle of the flat part of the test. Inside the mouth are sharp teeth. The urchin uses them to grind up plant food.

Sharp spines

The test of a sea urchin is covered in sharp spines. When people swim or paddle in the sea, they sometimes step on the spines and hurt themselves. The spines fall off when the sea urchin dies.

Walking on Stilts

A sea urchin usually moves using hundreds of tiny tube-shaped feet on the bottom of its test. Each foot has a sucker that grips on to rocks on the seafloor. The urchin can also move over rocks using its spines like stilts.

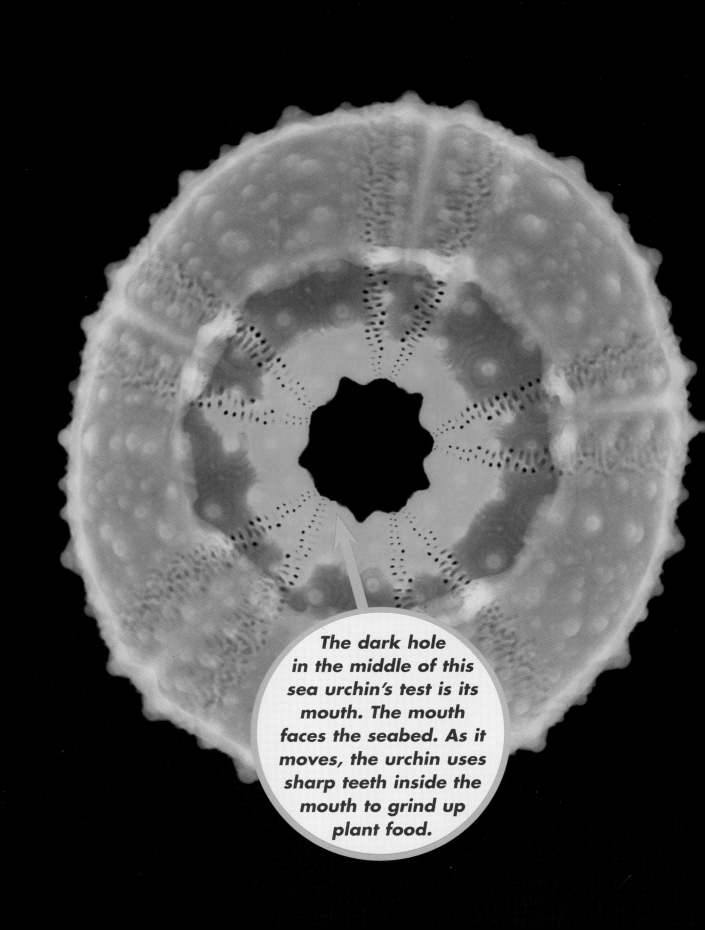

The dark hole in the middle of this sea urchin's test is its mouth. The mouth faces the seabed. As it moves, the urchin uses sharp teeth inside the mouth to grind up plant food.

Sea Worms

Sea creatures called *Mystacocarida* belong to the same family of animals as crabs and shrimps. They are all crustaceans. Most crustaceans live in water—either in freshwater rivers and lakes or in the ocean. All crustaceans have hard shells to support their bodies and protect their soft insides.

Sandy Home

***Mystacocarida* lives in shallow waters by the coast. It is found under the seafloor. *Mystacocarida* swims in the water between large grains of sand. It eats specks of food that float in this water. It sifts the specks from the water like a sieve.**

Body shape

Mystacocarida has a small head and a long trunk. The trunk is split into many parts, like the body of an earthworm. The head has two feelers, a mouth, and biting mouthparts to crush food. *Mystacocarida* is blind. It uses its feelers to move around.

Gone Fishing

The skin of a fish is made up of two layers. The outer layer is called the epidermis. The epidermis protects the body. It contains blood vessels, nerves, and organs that tell the fish about its surroundings. The dermis is the layer of skin under the epidermis.

Scaly skin

The scales of a fish grow from the dermis. The scales grow bigger as the fish grows older. Each year, a ring is added to each scale. Scientists count the rings on the scales to tell the age of the fish.

Eye to Eye

Flatfish such as sole begin life with an eye on each side of the head. As they grow older, flatfish take to the seafloor. The fish lays on one side, with one side of the body facing the seafloor. As the fish develops, one of the eyes moves around the head to the upper side of the body.

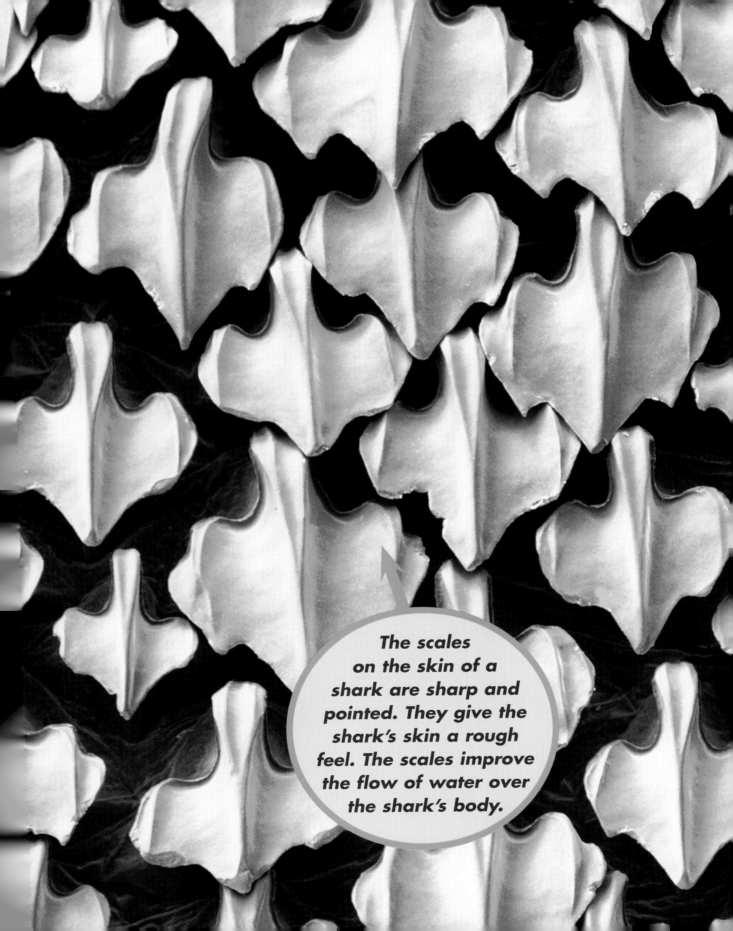

The scales on the skin of a shark are sharp and pointed. They give the shark's skin a rough feel. The scales improve the flow of water over the shark's body.

Body Bristles

Bristleworms belong to the same family as the earthworms. Bristleworms live in the ocean in rocky or sandy beaches. The worms get their name from the stiff bristles that line the sides of the body. The bristles grow in pairs and poke out through a row of bumps along the body.

Living Forest

Some bristleworms build sandy dens on the ocean floor. When the bristleworm's body is inside the burrow, its long feelers poke out through the surface. A group of worms in their burrows look like tiny forests of palm trees on the seafloor.

Bristleworm home

Bristleworms live in many different places in the ocean. Some hide among plankton or under rocks and stones. Others drill holes in rocks. Bristleworms also build dens in the sandy seafloor, poking out the head and feelers to gather floating food.

Glossary

cartilage: a firm, rubbery substance that forms the skeletons of sharks as well as your ears and nose.

cells: tiny building blocks that make up the bodies of all living creatures.

chemical: any substance found in nature or made by people.

chlorophyll: the green coloring that plants use to make their own food.

dermis: the inner layer of the skin.

echinoderms: a group of ocean animals with many tube feet, a hard test, and protective spines. Starfish, sand dollars, and sea urchins are echinoderms.

epidermis: the outer layer of the skin.

plankton: tiny creatures that drift freely in the oceans and are food for many animals.

silica: the hard, glassy chemical that makes up the cell walls of some ocean plants.

streamlined: having a body with a smooth shape that moves easily through air or water.

test: a hard shell that protects and supports the bodies of ocean animals such as sea urchins.

tube feet: the tiny tubelike "feet" that an echinoderm uses to move around.

Further Study

Books

Ganeri, Anita. *Oceans (Curious Kids Guides)*. New York: Kingfisher, 2002.

Kranking, Kathleen W., and Norbert Wu. *The Ocean Is...* New York: Henry Holt and Co., 2003.

Rivera, Shiela. *Ocean (First Step Nonfiction)*. Minneapolis, Minnesota: Lerner Publishing Group, 2005.

Rudy, Lisa Jo. *Ocean Life (Learn All About)*. New York: Teaching Resources (Scholastic), 2003.

Wade, Laura. *Knowledge Masters: Sea and Sea Life*. London UK, Chrysalis Children's Books, 2004.

Web sites

www.enchantedlearning.com/coloring/oceanlife.shtml
The Enchanted Learning web site features hundreds of fun activities, crafts, and games to help you learn about all sorts of different life in the oceans.

www.mbayaq.org/lc/activities.asp
The Monterey Bay Aquarium's web site is packed full of fun games and learning activities.

Index